OLIVER FIBS
Written & Illustrated by Barbara Alger
Edited by: Thom Hazaert

Oliver Fibs moved from London to Greece
with a trunk full of cash and Rowena his niece.
Then he purchased some land
by a stream on a hill, where he built a big house,
and a very fine mill.

Soon Oliver learned to make flour from grain.
He would bag it and tag it
and he'd never complain.
It appeared he had all that a man could desire.
And yet tragically,
'Oliver Fibs was a liar'
spreading fables and fiction
and tales of deceit,
spinning yarns of deception
while he ground up his wheat.

Now the summer was hot
and the air was too dry
when a stranger in red
seemed to just happen by.
Riding his horse to the top of that hill,
and making his way into Oliver's mill.

"My name is Falafel Kastoolus The Grand,"
he said with a grin as he stuck out his hand.
"I'm here for a sack of your very best flour.
But you must make it quick,
I have less than one hour!"

"Certainly!" Oliver said with a jerk.
"Come into the mill,
you can watch while I work."
The water wheel spinning
and grinding and squeaking,
Falafel Kastoolus The Grand
started speaking.

He bragged about riches.
He talked about wealth.
He spoke of a dish he created himself.
"Falafels" He called them,
bursting with pride,
patties with chickpeas and spices inside.
He said they went perfect
with yogurt and honey.
He said that he sold them
and he made lots of money!

But Oliver Fibs never heard what was said.
He was too busy thinking up lies in his head.

"Did you know?"
He began with a dishonest boast.
**"That my all-purpose flour
makes award winning toast."**

**"Did I mention the fact I can stand on my head,
while I grind enough wheat
to make ten loaves of bread?"**

**"Did I tell you" he asked
while he bounced on his heel,
"That my grandfather's father
invented the wheel?"**

Then one final lie fell from Oliver's lips
as he lifted that bag full of flour to his hips.
"Did I tell you?"
He lied to Falafel The Grand.
**"That I've discovered a way
to make flour from sand?"**
But the stranger in red simply lifted his hat.
He was going to be late.
There was no time to chat.
So, he picked up his flour.
They exchanged their goodbyes.
And he went on his way,
still believing those lies.

Now a month came and went,
but it came without rain.
The ground became parched
and it killed all the grain.
The people were starving,
they needed more wheat.
But the crops were destroyed
by the drought and the heat.

So, Falafel Kastoolus
returned to the mill.
He came with an army;
they stood on the hill.
They stood there with axes
and pitch forks and knives.
"We must feed our children!
We must feed our wives!
Our families are starving!
Our kids need to eat!"
They screamed and they shouted.
"We came here for wheat!"

"Our people are starving all over this land!"
Screamed Falafel Kastoolus
with a torch in his hand.
"You told me yourself;
you can turn sand into flour.
I command you," he said,
"to make use of that power!
You must make enough flour
for every person in Greece,
or you'll pay for your lie,
with the life of your niece!"

Poor sweet Rowena
felt sickened and sad.
A horrible plague took her mom and her dad.
Oliver Fibs was the only family she had.
**"But the people of Greece
had a right to be mad."**
She thought to herself
as she cried, and she cried.
She knew right away that her uncle had lied.
She knew he could never
make flour from sand.
He had broken her heart.
She did not understand.

So, Oliver Fibs sat alone on that hill,
in the still of the night,
on the stoop of his mill,
moaning and groaning, regretting his lie,
sickened and sorry, he started to cry!

He cried, and he cried,
and he cried, and he cried.

"Why, oh why, oh why had he lied?"
He thought to himself,
in the drought, in the heat.
**"I'm a miller by trade. I'm a grinder of wheat.
Perhaps,"** he surmised,
**"by the skill of my hand,
I could learn to make flour
out of nothing but sand."**

So, Oliver Fibs hurried off to the shore.
He filled buckets of sand
until his muscles got sore.
Then he carted that sand
to his very own mill,
where he started to grind it
just using his skill.

With a shovel, a pail,
and the water wheel turning,
the gears started grinding,
the belts started burning.
The mill that surrounded
him filled up with smoke.
And then everything stopped.
THE GRINDING WHEEL BROKE!

Oliver Fibs gave a quivering pout.
He started to cry, then he started to shout.
"Oh, how can I save her?"
"Oh, what can I do?"
Then he ripped out his hair
for a moment or two,
falling hard on his knees
much too weary to stand,
he wept and he wept
leaving tears in the sand.

But while he was kneeling there
helplessly bawling,
the teeniest tiniest voice started calling.
It was angry and shrill,
an unusual pitch.
It came from the sand;
it was the voice of a witch.
"Hey, You!"
The witch shouted with a scowl and a twitch,
scratching her head because sand made it itch.
"What is your problem? "
She said with a roar.
"Where is the water?"
"Where is the shore?"
"Why have you stolen my house in the sand?
Tell me right now!"
She said, scratching her hand.

But Oliver Fibs didn't hear that old witch
ranting and raving in such a high pitch.
Because Oliver Fibs was still lost in despair,
With his knees in the sand,
and his butt in the air.

So, the witch spoke again.
her voice booming and brash,
shaking her finger and scratching her rash.

"Why have you stolen my house in the sand?
You have such a nice house,
and such beautiful land."

Poor Oliver sat there with sand in his clothes.
It was stuffed in his pockets.
It was stuck up his nose.
It was in every eyelash and stuffed in his ears.
But he answered that witch
through his sand covered tears.

He explained why he'd taken
her house in the sand.
How he'd foolishly lied to a powerful man.
And because of that lie
they had taken his niece,
and locked her away
in a prison in Greece.

"Well" said the Sand Witch,
as she steadied her stand.
**"I'll be happy to help you
make flour from sand.
But in exchange,"**
Said the witch, as she stuck out her hand,
**"You must give me your mill,
and your house,
and your land."**

Well, Oliver Fibs started dancing in place.
Then he kissed that old witch
with the rash on her face.
He was happy, and giddy,
He was willing indeed!
He stuck out his hand
and he quickly agreed!

So, the Sand Witch started chanting,
and ranting and twitching,
using one hand for magic
and the other for itching.
She pointed her finger
and jiggled her hand
making mountains of flour
from nothing but sand.

So, when Falafel Kastoolus returned to the mill,
he saw mountains of flour
all over that hill!
An ocean of goodness
to bake and devour,
he closed his eyes tight,
he jumped into that flour,
he sang songs about pastries
and cinnamon toast.
When he finally got up
he looked just like a ghost!
He got into his wagon.
He traveled through Greece.
He fed all the people, freed Oliver's niece,
went back to his house, got out of the heat,
and made a gigantic falafel to eat.

The lovely Rowena was safely returned.
Oliver hugged her, his lesson was learned.
He promised Rowena with tears in his eyes,
he was done being boastful,
he was done telling lies!
He had lost his big house
by the stream on a hill.
He lost all his land.
He lost his fine mill.
But he still had the love
of his beautiful niece.
He was the happiest unemployed
miller in Greece!

The Sand Witch still lives
in that house on the hill.
She makes excellent flour
in Oliver's mill.
Her skin doesn't itch
because she sleeps in a bed.
And she makes a good living,
selling, '**Sand Witch Bread**'.

Wondervilleroad com
Wondervilleroad@gmail.com